EXPERIMENT WITH LIGHT

Written by **Bryan Murphy**

Science Consultant Dr Christine Sutton
Nuclear Physics Department, University of Oxford
Education Consultant Ruth Bessant

Scholastic Canada Ltd
123 Newkirk Rd, Richmond Hill, Ontario, Canada

First published in Great Britain in 1991 by Two-Can Publishing Ltd,
27 Cowper Street, London EC2A 4AP.

4321   Printed in Italy by Amadeus – Rome   1234/9

Canadian Cataloguing in Publication Data
Murphy, Bryan
        Experiment with Light
        Includes Index
        ISBN 0–590–73883–6

    1. Light – Experiments – Juvenile literature.
        I. Kindberg, Sally.   II. Pragoff, Fiona
                III. Title

QC360.M87   1991   j535'.078   C91–093845–8

All photographs except those on p.15 are copyright © Fiona Pragoff, and except for the following: Cover ZEFA Picture Library (UK) Ltd p.4 (top) ZEFA Picture Library (UK) Ltd (bottom left) J. Allan Cash Photolibrary (bottom right) Science Photo Library p.5 (bottom right) NHPA p.7 (centre right) J. Allan Cash Photolibrary p.10 (top) Science Photo Library (centre left) Art Directors Photo Library (bottom) NHPA p.11 (top) ZEFA Picture Library (UK) Ltd p.12 (top) ZEFA Picture Library (UK) Ltd p.22 (top) NHPA (bottom left) Telegraph Colour Library (bottom right) ZEFA Picture Library (UK) Ltd p.23 (top) ZEFA Picture Library (UK) Ltd p.26 (top right) Science Photo Library p.28 (top right) ZEFA Picture Library (UK) Ltd

All illustrations by Sally Kindberg. Edited by Monica Byles

Thanks to the staff and pupils of St Thomas' C.E. Primary School, London W10. Thanks also to Matthew Dickens and Pippa West

CONTENTS

All words marked in **bold** can be found in the glossary

WHAT IS LIGHT?

Light is very strange. You cannot taste it, feel it, hear it or smell it – but you can see it. Here are some interesting light facts.

Light moves very fast. In one second, a beam of light can travel the same distance as going around the world seven times.

▶ Light is a form of **energy**. This house uses solar panels to convert the sun's rays to make energy to light the household.

▲ When something gets hot, it gives out light. Very hot things like glowing coals in a fire give out red light.

▲ Extremely hot things like these stars give out bright white light. Their colour depends on their surface temperature.

▼ **Transparent** things, like clear water, allow light to pass straight through them.

▶ **Translucent** things, like frosted glass, scatter light as it passes through them so that they look blurred.

You cannot see through **opaque** things because light is not able to go through them.

▶ The energy in sunlight is used by green plants to make food. Both humans and animals eat plants and take in some of this energy.

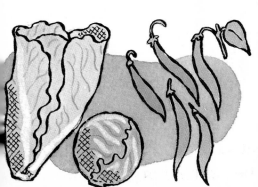

SUNDIALS AND ECLIPSES

Have you ever played a game with your **shadow?** On a bright day, the sun casts a shadow of you on the ground. Light travels in straight lines, so where it is blocked by your solid body, a shadow falls. Is the shadow exactly the same shape as your body or different? Why do you think this is?

◄ Is your shadow lying towards the sun or away from it? Keep still and ask a friend to draw around your shadow and colour it in with chalk. See what happens to the shape of your shadow if it falls on an upright wall instead of on to the flat ground.

Shadows do not keep still. As the sun moves across the sky, shadows must move as well. You can make a shadow clock or **sundial** to tell the time. All you need is a pencil, some modelling clay and some cardboard.

Poke the end of the pencil in the modelling clay and fasten it near the edge of the cardboard so that it stands upright. This is your sundial.

Put the sundial on a sunny windowsill. The sun will cast a shadow of the pencil on to the cardboard. Every hour, mark off the position of the shadow. At the end of the day, you will have a clock that never needs winding!

Remember never to look directly at the sun. Its brightness can hurt your eyes.

Sometimes, the sun casts very big shadows on the earth. If the moon gets in the way of the sun, the sun looks very strange indeed. All you can see is the outline of the sun shining around the edge of the dark moon. This is called an **eclipse**.

Indoors, you can use shadows to make a picture called a **silhouette**. Cast a shadow of a friend on a wall with a lamp. If you carefully stick a piece of paper to the wall you can draw around the shadow. Your friend must keep very still. When you have finished, either cut out the shape, or colour it in. Even though there is no detail, it should be easy to tell whose shape it is.

7

A NAILHOLE CAMERA

Have you ever wanted to draw perfectly? A nailhole **camera** will help you trace a scene on to paper so that you can colour it in later. You need only cheap materials – an empty box, black paint, tracing paper, tape or glue, some black cloth and of course, a nail.

Cut a rectangular hole from one side of the box leaving 2 centimetres of box around the edges. Paint the inside of the box black. Now ask an adult to make a small hole with the nail in the middle of the side facing the large hole. When the paint has dried, seal the top of the box tightly and loosely tape or glue the tracing paper over the big hole.

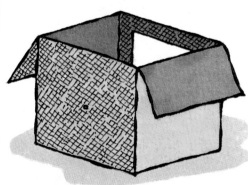

▲ Rest the camera on a steady surface. Now point the nailhole at a bright scene. The picture, or image, you see is upside-down but you can now trace it.

To see the picture better, drape the dark cloth as a hood over the side with the tracing paper, then over your head. Move the box to get a clearer image.

8

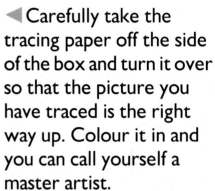

◀ Carefully take the tracing paper off the side of the box and turn it over so that the picture you have traced is the right way up. Colour it in and you can call yourself a master artist.

◀ Try making nailhole cameras with boxes of different sizes and with smaller or larger holes. If you make the nailhole bigger, the picture will be brighter, but it might be a little fuzzy.

9

BENDING LIGHT

Nearly all the light on the earth comes from the sun. Even moonlight is sunlight that has bounced off the moon. Can you think of any other sources of light?

▲ Try looking at the stars on a very clear night. It looks as though they are twinkling. This is because light shining in straight lines from the stars is bent by changing air currents in the atmosphere.

◀ On very hot days, there is a layer of hot air near the ground. Sometimes this can bend the light and look like a reflection floating in mid-air, called a **mirage**. Can you see one behind the horses?

◀ The next time you go swimming underwater, look up at the surface. It looks as though there is a mirror floating on the water. This is because the rays of light from above have bent where they meet the water.

▼ Here is another trick that works by bending light. Place a counter or button on the bottom of an opaque cup and position a friend just far enough distant so that he cannot quite see the counter. Start filling the cup with water and the counter will magically appear to him.

LIGHT AND LENSES

Many scientists make use of magnifying instruments such as **microscopes** to investigate tiny objects. You may have a magnifying glass at home to help you look at small insects more closely. **Magnifying glasses** are thicker in the middle than at the edges and can make things look larger.

What would you see through a lens that is thinner in the middle than at the edges? You can find out by looking through the **glasses** of a short-sighted person. Can you see the difference? Everything looks smaller. Never wear someone else's glasses for too long.

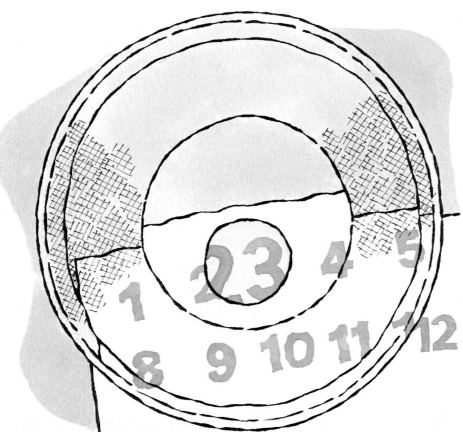

◀ Here is an experiment to make your own magnifying glass. You will need a transparent shallow dish or beaker, water and some oil. Pour some water into the dish or beaker and carefully float a little oil on the surface to form a small slick about one centimetre across.

Now put the dish on to some printed type. If you look through the oil, the type looks bigger. Try focusing the magnifying glass by making the water deeper or shallower.

SNAP HAPPY

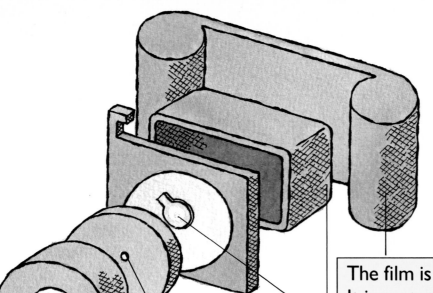

Do you have a camera of your own? If not, ask an adult if you can look at one to see how it works. Compare it to a nailhole camera. What changes can you see?

◄ Cameras come in all shapes and sizes but almost all of them have five parts.

The film is where the image is focused. It is coated in sensitive chemicals.

The lens is a piece of curved glass or plastic. The light is focused through the lens to make an image on the film.

The aperture is a hole which can be altered in size to let in more light. On a dark day the hole must be larger.

A lightproof box forms the heart of any camera. It is usually black inside to absorb stray light.

The shutter controls the length of time that the light hits the film.

◄ Automatic cameras make all the adjustments themselves.

► A photographer has more control over his or her picture if he or she uses a camera that has to be set by hand.

Here are some tips to help you take even better pictures. Many scientists use photographs to keep a long-lasting record of their observations.

- Remember to take off the lens cap!

- Make sure there is enough light if you are not using a flash.

- If your camera needs focusing, be very accurate.

- Keep your hands very still.

- Make sure that your subject fills the frame.

- Make sure heads, feet and hands are in shot.

- Keep your fingers away from the lens, or you are likely to ruin some of your best shots.

- Make sure the film is wound on properly.

- Do not point the camera at the sun. The sun should always be kept behind you.

FOCUS ON EYES

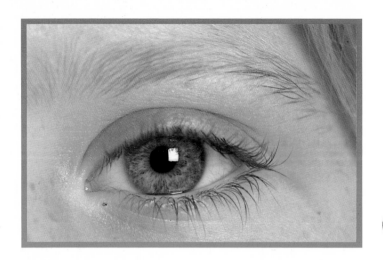

You can see by using your **eyes**. They are a bit like cameras.

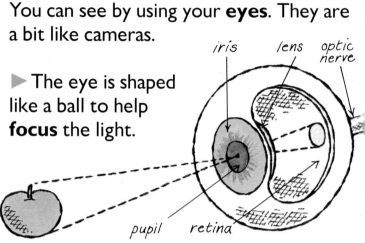

▶ The eye is shaped like a ball to help **focus** the light.

iris lens optic nerve

pupil retina

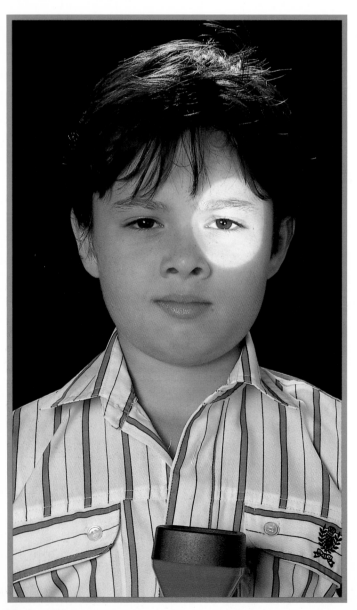

◀ Draw the curtains in the room and turn off any lights. Look at one of your friend's eyes. How big is the pupil? Now carefully shine the flashlight at it and see what happens. Did the pupil change size? When it is dark, the pupil grows bigger to let more light in. When it is bright, the pupil gets smaller because it does not need so much light to see.

The light gets into the eye through the pupil, the black hole in the middle.

You have a lens in your eye to focus the light on to the retina. Sometimes this lens does not work properly and people need to wear an extra lens in the form of glasses or contact lenses.

The image is focused upside-down on to the retina instead of on to film. The optic nerve carries the message to your brain, which turns the image right way up.

The iris, or coloured part, controls the light going into the eye by changing the size of the pupil. Look at a friend's eyes with the help of a flashlight.

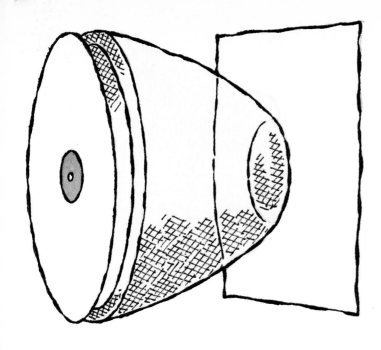

You can make a good model of the eye using a round bowl made of clear glass and some cardboard. Cut a pupil about one centimetre in diameter in the cardboard. You might like to paint a coloured iris around it. Point your model eye towards a television.

Hold a retina made from a sheet of white paper behind the eye. Move the model eye backwards and forwards until you can see a good image of the television on the paper retina. Remember, the image will be upside-down.

OPTICAL ILLUSIONS

You can fool your brain by looking at optical illusions. Some look very strange indeed. Optical illusions play a trick on your brain about what you think you see.

▶ Hold this page about 30 centimetres from your face and close your left eye. Look straight at the ant. You can still see the spider. Now, without taking your eye off the ant, slowly bring the page closer to your face. Suddenly the spider will disappear! You have found your 'blind spot' where the optic nerve joins the eye to take messages to the brain.

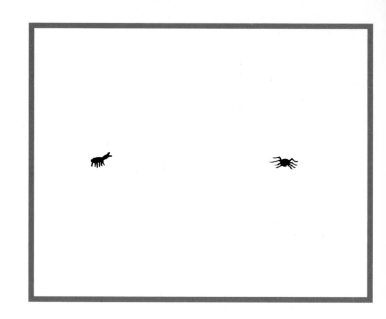

▼ What are these two friends looking at?

▼ Will the girl ever reach the top of this staircase?

▼ Which boy is the tallest?

▼ Can you see ghostly grey dots where the white lines meet?

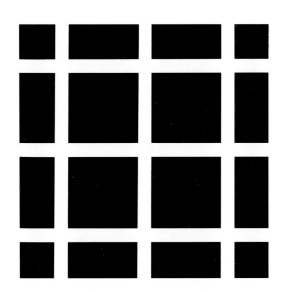

▼ A flight of steps, from above or below?

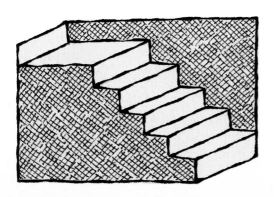

▲ Does the frame hold the portrait of a beautiful young lady wearing earrings or of an old lady with a large nose?

MIRROR MAGIC

Whenever light hits something very flat and shiny like a **mirror**, it bounces off. This is called **reflecting**. When light reflects off a mirror, some strange things can happen. Mirrors are great fun.

They can be very useful as well. The mirrors on a car are placed in the centre of the windshield and on the front wings of the car so that the driver can see the position of all the vehicles on the road behind him without needing to twist around in his seat.

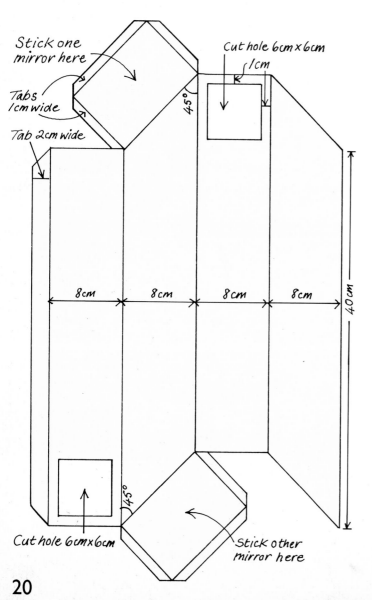

Stick one mirror here

Tabs 1cm wide

Tab 2cm wide

Cut hole 6cm x 6cm

1cm

45°

8cm   8cm   8cm   8cm

40 cm

Cut hole 6cm x 6cm

45°

Stick other mirror here

Do you sometimes wish that you could see over a wall without climbing it? You can do so by using two small mirrors to make a **periscope**. All you need are the two mirrors, about 10 x 8 centimetres, and some cardboard. Ask an adult to help you make it.

◀ Draw this shape on to cardboard and cut it out. Stick the mirrors in position, apply glue to the tabs, then fold the cardboard into a long box shape.

▶ Now you can look around corners and over walls without being seen – very useful for games of hide and seek.

Look for other mirrors at home. Some are flat and some are curved. A spoon is like a mirror. Look at your strange reflection in the front and back of its bowl. Which side makes you look upside-down?

20

THE COLOURS OF THE RAINBOW

Imagine if the whole world looked black and white. There would be grey skies, grey grass and grey flowers. Everything would be grey. **Colours** are not just pretty. Many animals and plants use colours. Sometimes a flower needs to stand out, so that it is noticed by insects that come to spread its pollen.

▼ The males of many species of animals and birds, like this beautiful peacock, use bright colours to attract a partner.

▲ Other animals use their skin or feathers to hide from their enemies. Chameleons can change their colour to match their background.

Rainbow colours

red

orange

yellow

green

blue

indigo

violet

▲ The light that comes from the sun is made of many colours, all mixed together. If the sun is shining and it is raining at the same time, the different colours in the sunlight are split up. Then you can see a huge arc of colour called a **rainbow**.

◀ You can make your own rainbow if you are watering the garden on a sunny day. Put your finger over the end of the hosepipe to make a very fine spray. If you stand with the sun behind you, you can see all the colours of the rainbow in the spray.

Grass looks green because it reflects green light. It soaks in all the other colours. A red apple looks red because it reflects red light. On a sunny day, black things get hot because they soak in all colours. White things stay cooler because they reflect all colours.

23

COLOUR DISCS

What do you think would happen if you mixed together all the colours of the rainbow?

Cut out a circle from cardboard and divide it into six equal segments. Colour them red, orange, yellow, green, blue and purple. Make two holes, each one centimetre apart at the middle of the disc and loop about 50 centimetres of string through them. Tie the ends together and hook the string over your middle fingers. You can now spin the disc very quickly by pulling the string and slackening it when it has unwound. The disc will wind the string again so you can spin it faster and faster.

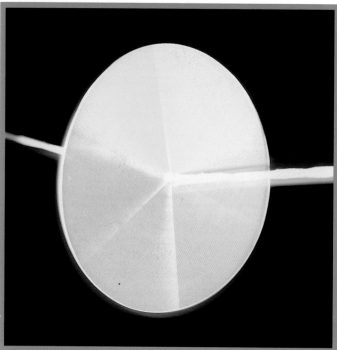

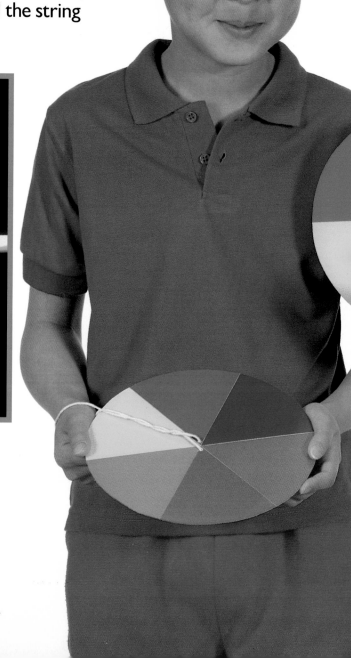

▲ What does the disc look like when it is spinning quickly? Can you see all the colours? Instead of looking colourful, the disc now looks greyish-white. This is because the speed of the spinning disc blurs the separate colours so that your eyes are confused and mix them together.

▼ On the other side of the disc, divide it up into three segments and colour them red, green and blue. Does this also look greyish-white when it spins? Try some more discs with two colours on them. Try red and green, red and blue, then blue and green. What colour does each spinning disc look like?

WORLDS WITHOUT COLOUR

Some people cannot see some colours very well. They are called **colour blind**. Most people who are colour blind cannot see the difference between the different shades of red and green. Can you see any numbers in this circle? People with red and green colour blindness cannot see them.

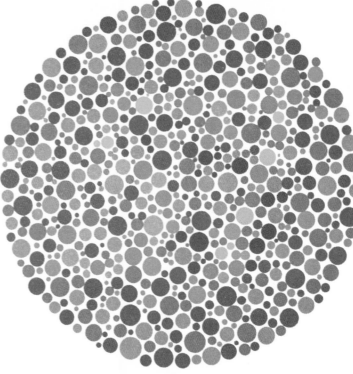

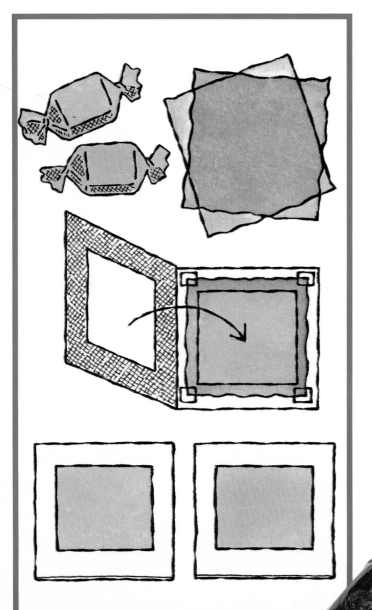

◀ Another way of seeing colour is to look through some thin coloured plastic called a **filter**. You can collect many different filters from candy wrappers. Mount them in cardboard frames. Try looking through a red one. Anything that is red, yellow or orange should look light, while other colours look dark. What does the sky look like? Photographers often use a red or orange filter when they take pictures of the countryside, to make the sky darker.

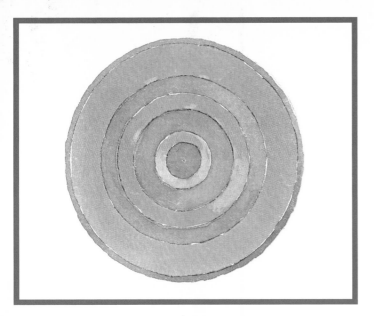

Put a green filter in front of your left eye and a red one in front of your right eye. Look at these pictures with one eye closed then the other. They look very strange. Try drawing your own red and green pictures.

COLOUR TELEVISION

Have you ever thought how a **television** picture is made? The next time you are watching your favourite program, have a good look at the screen.

▼ The picture is made up of little dots. Can you see what colours they are? There are only red, green and blue dots. How can all the different colours you see in a television picture be made up of just three colours?

Mixing paints

red + green = brown

green + blue = turquoise

red + blue = purple

red + green + blue = black

If you move away from the screen, the light from the different dots mixes to produce the colours of the picture.

► Mixing paints is not like mixing light. Red and green paints mix to look brown. Red and green light look yellow. Can you see any other differences on the opposite page?

28

A red part of the picture only has the red dots glowing. A blue part of the picture only has the blue dots glowing. A green part of the picture only has the green dots glowing.

A turquoise part of the picture has the green and blue dots glowing.

A purple part of the picture has the red and blue dots glowing.

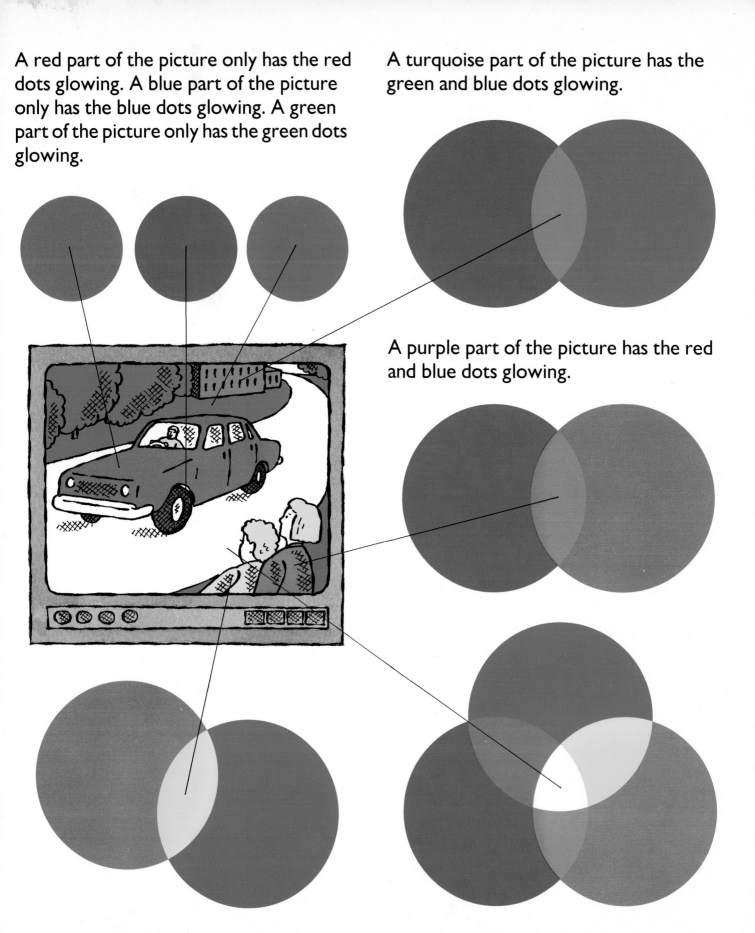

A yellow part of the picture has the red and green dots glowing.

A white part would have all three dots glowing, red, blue and green.

GLOSSARY

Camera is a machine that takes photographs by focusing light on to paper coated with light-sensitive chemicals.

Colour is the different way things look because they reflect different parts of sunlight or electric light. These parts are separated in the bands of a rainbow.

Colour blindness is when a person is unable to see the difference between certain colours such as red and green.

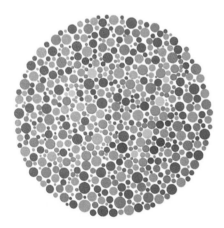

Eclipse is when the light from the sun is shadowed by the moon or a planet for a short time.

Energy is needed by all things to be active.

Eyes sense light radiating from objects and pass messages to the brain so that we see.

Glasses are lenses that many people wear in front of their eyes so that they can focus properly. Some people may wear contact lenses on the surface of their eyes instead of glasses.

Magnifying glass is a lens that makes small things look bigger.

Microscope uses two or more lenses to make very small things look much bigger.

Mirages are seen when light is bent by hot air. Some mirages look like puddles. They are most often seen in hot places like deserts.

Mirror is a shiny surface that reflects light.

Opaque things do not let light through.

Optical illusion is a trick on our brains about what we think we see.

Periscope uses two mirrors to bounce light over objects such as high walls. They are used in submarines to see above the surface of the waves.

Rainbow is made when light goes through a raindrop, and comes out as separate colours. Sometimes we can see these colours in the sky.

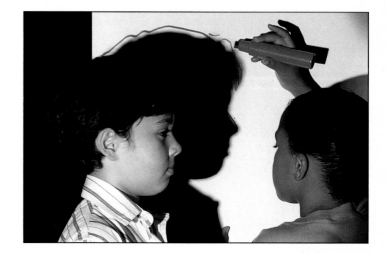

Reflecting is when light is bounced off a shiny surface.

Shadow is the dark area cast by an object that is in front of a light source.

Silhouette is a shadow picture.

Sundial (shadow clock) is an instrument to tell the time from the position of the sun's shadow on a time face, traditionally carved into a stone surface outdoors.

Television is a machine that displays the sounds and pictures sent through the air from TV stations.

Translucent things scatter light as it passes through them.

Transparent things let light pass straight through them, so that they look clear.

INDEX

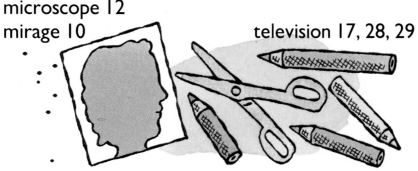